J
Our Way

'He is not here – he has been raised!'

Mark 16: 6

The Benedictine Nuns
of Turvey Abbey

Additional material by Mark Poulter

McCrimmons
Great Wakering Essex England

First published in 2000 by
McCRIMMON PUBLISHING CO LTD
10-12 High Street, Great Wakering, Essex SS3 0EQ
Telephone: 01702 218956
Fax: 01702 216082
Email: mccrimmons@dial.pipex.com
Web site: www.mccrimmons.co.uk

Jesus, Our Way ISBN 0 85597 613 6

Jesus, Our Light ISBN 0 85597 611 X
Jesus, Our Hope ISBN 0 85597 612 8

Edited and additional information by Mark Poulter
All images are taken from original paintings by the Benedictine Nuns of Turvey Abbey, part of the *Jesus, Our Life series of posters.*
Typeset in Frutiger Light 11.5/13.5pt, 10/12pt and ITC Fenice Regular Italic 24/26pt
Printed by Thanet Press Ltd., Margate, Kent

Contents

Jesus, Our Way

The final events in the life of Jesus

Introduction

The stunning set of 12 posters which accompany this book follows the final events in the life of Jesus, beginning with his triumphant entry into Jerusalem. Following the Last Supper, his arrest and crucifixion, the later images reflect the appearances of the risen Jesus to his disciples in the weeks after the resurrection. This set shows the way in which Jesus leads us: through suffering and death to the glory of the Resurrection and the coming of the Holy Spirit.

Using this booklet

This book is designed to help teachers, catechists, R.E. co-ordinators and others to make the most of these beautiful images. On each page the artist has sought to describe her inspiration for each painting by reflecting on the relevant scripture references. We have also included:

- a picture of the poster;
- a quote from scripture; and,
- questions for discussion.

Page 31 of this booklet includes a cross-reference to themes and topics, such as those included in popular education programmes like *Here I Am* and *Walk With Me*. You may also wish to use some of the ideas that follow.

Discussion and teaching

The Questions for Discussion included in this booklet are designed to help teachers and catechists develop the responses of children to these well-known Bible stories. If you have time, we suggest you look up the scriptural reference yourself and reflect on it. Why not use a piece of the text as a heading for a display or a starting point for a session? And if you are stuck for time, you may want to use the scriptural quote we have selected. We do not aim to offer formulaic lessons and hope you will adapt and alter the material to suit the needs of the children in your care.

Display and decoration

The vibrant and striking colours of the paintings means they are ideally suited to display in Church, on notice-boards, as the centre piece of an R.E. display or prayer table/altar, or around school. You may wish to copy or type out one or more of the Questions for Discussion on each page and arrange them with the poster/s to make your displays more interactive and appealing to children and adults alike.

Assemblies and services

The posters are deal for use in assemblies and services. You may want to display them as a basis for discussion or as a stimulus for prayer or reflection. They will also add colour and meaning to Bible stories read or acted out in the parish or school.

Prayer and meditation

A striking visual image often helps people to pray, meditate or reflect. You could use one or more of the posters as a focal point for an altar/prayer table or as the centre piece of a prayer service. This set of posters is particularly suited to themes such as Death and New Life. As many of the pictures cover Lent and Easter, these images are appropriate to many of the Spring topics of popular R.E. programmes, such as Thanksgiving, Meals and Good News. (Please see page 31 for more themes.)

Creative writing and artwork

The rich and vivid colour of these illustrations, combined with the powerful imagery, makes them an ideal starting point for creative work. Why not use them to provoke thought and discussion before writing poetry or prayers? Or how about asking children to copy or re-design an image as part of their art work?

And finally...

Why not share your ideas and experiences with us?

We are always interested in finding out what works well and what materials you need to better fulfil your ministry.

Contact us at:
McCrimmons, Freepost CL2425, Great Wakering,
Southend-on-Sea, Essex, SS3 0BR.
01702-218956 (phone) 01702-216082 (fax)
mccrimmons@dial.pipex.com (email)
www.mccrimmons.co.uk (Web site)

You are on you way to Jerusalem with Jesus and one of the disciples.
The streets are crowded.
Listen to the people laughing and shouting. You have to listen very hard to hear what Jesus says.
Jesus stops and looks at you and says, "*Go to the village facing you, and you will at once find a tethered donkey and a colt. Untie them and bring them to me.*"

You look puzzled. What if somebody tries to stop you. Listen as Jesus reassures you, "*If anyone says anything to you, you are to say*, '*The master needs them and will send them back at once.*' " You walk towards the village.
Why has Jesus asked you to do this?

As you untie the donkey, you think about how close you have become.
Is Jesus going away? Is he going on a journey?

Jesus is waiting just where you left him. He looks calm, holds out his hand and takes the rein of the donkey. The other disciple is busy taking his cloak off and putting it on the donkey. The streets are full of people. Has anyone noticed that Jesus has climbed on the donkey?

Crowds of people are climbing the trees and cutting down the branches. Watch as they throw them to the ground. A small group of people next to you starts to sing loudly and soon everyone is joining in. "Hosanna, Hosanna to the king of David."

The donkey is making its way slowly through the crowds. The noise is getting louder and louder. Watch as some children start to dance and throw their palm branches in the air. Jesus looks back at the road covered in palm branches and cloaks. Where is he going? Must he journey alone?

Watch Jesus until he disappears from sight. How do you feel now?

1 Jesus enters Jerusalem

Matthew 21: 1-11; Mark 11: 1-11;
Luke 19: 28-44; John 12: 12-19

'Wild excitement' (NEB) surrounded Jesus as he entered the city, an apt description of what the tumult must have been like. It is rendered here in a festive riot of colours, the city decked out for a feast, but in the midst of it, Jesus is sad. All this enthusiasm lacks depth, they are very far from a change of heart. Because of this, Jesus will be unable to stop the great city from being destroyed. 'If only you had known on this great day the way that leads to peace.' (*Luke 19: 42*)

'God bless him who comes in the name of the Lord.'

Mark 11: 10

Questions for discussion

What things do you celebrate?

What do you enjoy about the celebrations?

What friends would you invite to your celebrations?

How do we know that Jesus was so popular?

Why is Jesus a special friend to you?

How can Jesus help you to become a better person?

Imagine that you are sitting on the steps of the temple. You have been there since early morning. You have watched the traders set up their stalls. You have watched more and more pilgrims arrive. The traders shout and laugh hoping that many pilgrims will come to their stall. You are sitting very still just watching and listening.

All of a sudden the shouting stops. The pigeons and doves settle in their cages and even the goat kids are still. Jesus is standing at the bottom of the Temple steps. Watch as he runs up the steps to the money changers. He pushes the table over. The sound of hundreds of coins falling to the ground fills the air. The money changers greedily try to grab the coins but Jesus pushes the tables again.

Next he goes to the dove sellers and flings the cages open. Listen to the squawks and watch the feathers as they fall to the ground. All eyes are on Jesus as he shouts telling the people that this should be a house of prayer and they have turned it into a bandit's den.

In silence the pilgrims climb the steps empty-handed. Crowds of people are making their way to Jesus in silence. These people are sick and they want Jesus to heal them. Watch as he heals them.

Something has broken the silence. It's the sound of children singing. Join in with their singing, "Hosanna, hosanna to the son of David." There are some chief priests outside the temple. They are angry. They know that Jesus has special power. How do you know that Jesus has special power?

2 *Jesus cleanses the temple*

Matthew 21: 12-17; Mark 11: 15-19;
Luke 19: 45-48; John 2: 13-22

This sadness was still with him when he entered the temple and found the precincts filled with the noisy bustle of a market day. He cries out in exasperation: 'My house is a house of prayer for all nations; (cf. *Mark 11: 17*; *Isaiah 56: 7*). Quoting Isaiah, Jesus points to the universal call of all peoples to God's Temple, an idea which did nothing to pacify his enemies.

'My temple will be called a house of prayer for the people of all nations.'

Mark 11: 17

Questions for discussion

Have you ever been to a market? What was it like?

Why was Jesus so unhappy about what was happening in the temple?

How do you know Jesus has special power?

What is your church like?

Do you like it when the church is quiet and still? Why?

Where do you go to pray?

Imagine that you are Peter.
You are sitting in the Upper room with Jesus and the other disciples.
Jesus is looking at each of the disciples.
He stops and looks at you.
You have gathered together many times but this time is different.

Watch as Jesus stands up from the table. He is carrying a jug of water and a towel. What is he going to do?

Jesus is starting to wash the feet of the disciples. As you watch you hear again the sound of the crowds singing, "Hosanna, hosanna to the son of David."

Look down and see Jesus kneeling at your feet now. What do you want to say to him? Jesus looks at you and says, "*If I do not wash you, you have no part in me.*"

Jesus starts to wash your feet and as you feel the cool water touching your skin you watch Jesus; and you think of the times that those hands have healed the sick, lifted small children and unrolled the scroll of the Torah in the synagogue. Tonight those hands are doing the work of a servant.

Jesus has finished washing your feet. What do you want to say to him?

3 The Washing of the Feet

John 13: 2-17

This picture and the next are about our fellowship with Jesus. A two-fold celebration takes place: the washing of the feet and the giving of Christ's Body and Blood as food and drink – two aspects of our union with him: mystical and sacramental. Peter is protesting against Jesus doing the job of a slave. He is slow in learning that the Kingdom of God is the world turned upside down. Jesus is about to speak of the Vine and the branches, underpinning his action: we too should wash each other's feet, being the least, and so establish the life-giving bond of unity and love with Jesus and among ourselves. This incorporation comes about in our Baptism, of which the washing is a sign, through the Eucharist, and through recognising our continued need to renew our union with him 'in memory of him'.

'He poured some water into a basin and began to wash the disciples' feet.'

John 13: 4

Questions for discussion

How do you think the disciples felt when Jesus washed their feet?

At first, Peter did not want Jesus to wash him.
Why do you think this was?

Which people look after you?

When did you join God's family?

Why do you think water is used to baptise people?

What does it mean to be part of Jesus?

Imagine your are Peter. Jesus has asked you to prepare a room for the Passover. Passover is a very special feast. You know what to do. You have helped your mother since you were a small boy. As you arrange the room you think of the times you have spent with Jesus – happy times and sad times.

The feast has arrived at last. You have all gathered together as Jesus asked. You look at Jesus sitting at the head of the table. What is he thinking about?

You hear the words, "Blessed are you, Lord God of the universe." Somehow you know this is the last time you will say these words with Jesus.

Jesus looks around the table. His eyes stop on each one of you. As Jesus looks at you, you feel afraid and start to sing louder and louder. This should be a party but instead there is a feeling of sadness.

The room has gone quiet. Jesus' words seem to echo. "*One of you is going to betray me.*" What is Jesus saying? You are all friends. You all love him. Surely this is the way it should stay?
Now Jesus is holding a piece of unleavened bread in his hands. As he prays the prayers of thanksgiving you look at his hands. These are the hands that have touched and healed lepers. Hands that have reached out to you across the water, hands that have broken bread and shared fish.

"*Take it and eat. This is my body.*"

What is Jesus saying? How can you share his body?
You want to shout out, "How, how?"
In silence, you share the bread, wondering what it means. Watch as Jesus holds the cup of wine. "*Take it and drink. This is my blood.*"
All eyes are on Jesus as he passes the cup. Drink from the cup. When you have finished look at Jesus.
What do you want to say to him?

Ask Jesus what is going to happen to him. What does he say?

4 *The Last Supper*

Matthew 26: 20-30; Mark 14: 12-26;
Luke 22: 14-30; John 13: 18 – John 17: 26

Night is closing in. The archway through which Judas is fleeing into the darkness intersects with the light round Jesus' head: he is still calling him, loving him. The atmosphere at this last meal together is heavy with foreboding. All eyes are on the Master, fearful, not understanding. The disciples listen as he prays and talks, explaining the meaning of what he has just done, celebrating their union. Jesus has become their new Passover Lamb, ready to be slaughtered, total gift, total love, setting them an example. Later the disciples will remember and be fulfilled with overwhelming joy, a joy no-one will be able to take away (cf *John.16: 22*). But before that a crucial, shattering test will have to be undergone.

'This is my body which is given for you.'

Luke 22: 19

Questions for discussion

Can you think of some of your special memories.
Why are they important to you?

Have you had any special meals? Who was there?

What would you like to say thank you to God for?

How can you say thank you to other people?

How can you show God you are grateful for everything he has done for you?

Imagine you are leaving the Upper room. You are following Jesus.
Where will he lead you?
As you walk you sing together.
You sing of God and his mighty power to save his people.

You have reached the Garden of Olives. The air around you feels warm and heavy. You put your lamp down and look at the shadows it casts on the trunks of the olive trees.

Jesus turns to you and says, "*Stay here while I pray.*" Jesus always went away by himself to pray – away to a lonely hillside or out in a boat. Why has he brought you here?

Jesus has taken hold of your arm and says, "*Come and watch with me.*" What does he want? Follow Jesus and sit down where he shows you. You lean your back against the rough trunk of an ancient olive tree and stare out into the night.

Now watch Jesus. His lips are moving but there is no sound. He stretches his arms towards heaven and then falls to the ground. He calls out, "*Father remove this cup from me.*"

Your heart is beating faster. What does Jesus mean? It's hard to stand by and watch Jesus suffering.

You feel yourself getting warmer and more and more tired. Close your eyes and fall asleep. You wake up with a start. You can feel a hand on your shoulder.
It's Jesus. He looks at you and says, "*Could you not watch with me for one hour?*"

You want to leave the garden but something makes you stay.
Tell Jesus what it is that makes you want to stay with him.

5 *Agony in Gethsemane*

Matthew 26: 36-46; Mark 14: 32-42; Luke 22: 39-46

Jesus, the wonder worker, whom sea and wind and evil spirits obey, who has more than 12 legions of angels at his disposal (cf. *Matthew 26: 54*) appears in all the weakness of his humanity. All the horror of what is to come is battering down on him. The beam of light in the darkness of the olive grove suggests the full passover moon; it represents the consolation brought by the angel (cf. *Luke 22: 43*), the light of God's presence who even in his darkest hour will not abandon him. Jesus is here fighting the great struggle that will seal our fate.

'Stay here and keep watch.'

Mark 14: 34

Questions for discussion

Have you ever seen a friend who was upset or in need of help?

What was wrong?

What can you do to help them?

Are there some times when there is nothing you can do?

Jesus still needs your help now. What can you do to show him he is your friend?

Imagine you are sitting in the Garden of Olives. Dawn is beginning to break. Look up at the sky and watch as it changes colour. Through the knotted trunks of the olive trees you can see the glow of lamps.
They are getting closer.

Listen to the sound of footsteps on the dry ground.
All at once Jesus is surrounded by people carrying torches and weapons. The torches cast shadows on the face of Jesus. Watch as one man comes forward and kisses Jesus on the cheek. It's Judas. How can Judas do this? You want to shout out and stop him.

The men are holding Jesus tightly. He doesn't struggle.
Walk over to Jesus and say one last thing to him.

In silence the people walk away with their prisoner, Jesus.
Watch as they walk. Jesus turns and looks at you.
Will you ever see him again?

6 *Jesus is arrested*

Matthew 26: 47-56; Mark 14: 43-52; Luke 22: 47-53; John 18: 3-12

The mob of armed men was totally superfluous. Jesus surrenders of his own free will. He could have escaped, as he had done so many times. But this is his hour. Jesus pronounces his great YES to God (cf. *2 Corinthians 1: 19*). Large hands grab him, the power of darkness. The disciples, all willing to defend him by violent means, are at a loss when Jesus tells them not to intervene. They panic and take to their heels.

'If, then, you are looking for me, let these others go.'

John 18: 8

Questions for discussion

Have you ever let down a friend? What happened?

What do you do when you feel angry?

Is fighting a good way of solving arguments?

What else could you do instead?

Why did Jesus tell the disciples not to fight?

You've been gathering together spices to go and anoint the body of Jesus. It's early morning and still dark and you are making your way to the tomb where they laid Jesus. The jars of spices are heavy. Your heart is heavy too. It's hard for you to believe that Jesus is really dead.

As you walk you think of the times you have spent with Jesus. You think of all the things you have told him about yourself.

As you get closer to the tomb you realise the stone has been rolled away. Who has done this? You feel frightened and confused. You must tell the disciples. Perhaps they will know where you will find Jesus. You must find him.

You run to tell the disciples. Tell them what has happened. Do they believe you?

Simon Peter and John look anxious too. You watch as they start to run to the tomb. John has reached the tomb first. He bends down and sees the linen clothes that were used to wrap the body of Jesus.

You have stayed outside the tomb. You are crying. Why has this happened?
You don't want to go inside the tomb. Tell the disciples why you must find Jesus.

7 *The Resurrection*

Matthew 28: 1-15; Mark 16: 1-8;
Luke 24: 1-12; John 20: 1-10

The poster draws its symbolism from the Book of Revelation, (ch. *21-22*): the New Heaven and the New Earth, opened up for us by Jesus. There is the river of life, flowing from the throne of God and of the Lamb, image of the Spirit given to us in Baptism, the river through which we have passed with Jesus into the Promised Land. Trees of life grow on either side, whose leaves are for the health of the nations, for all the world. His life is our life, here and now, and eternally.

'He is not here – he has been raised!'

Mark 16: 6

Questions for discussion

What makes you frightened?

Have you ever lost something or someone?
How did you feel?

Do others always believe what you tell them?

How does it feel when you are telling the truth and no-one believes you?

How can you find Jesus in your life today?

Imagine you are Mary Magdalene.
You have been standing outside
the tomb of Jesus crying.
You decide to look inside. Perhaps
Jesus is still there after all.

It's dark in the tomb, except for
two shining figures sitting where
the body of Jesus lay. The figures look at you and say, "*Why are you crying?*"
Tell them why you are so upset.

You can feel someone standing behind you. Turn around and see who it is.
He also wants to know. "*Why are you crying?*" Tell him why.

You ask the man to tell you where they have put the body of Jesus.
He must be the gardener. You turn away from the man because you are crying.
As you turn he calls your name, "*Mary.*"

You recognise the voice. It's Jesus! You have found him at last! Run to him and take hold of his arm. You are going to make sure you don't lose him again.
But Jesus looks at you and says, "*Do not cling to me.*" You let go of his arm. What does he mean?

Speak to Jesus and tell him how important it was for you to find him.

Now leave the garden and run to tell the disciples what has happened.
Will they believe you?

8 Jesus appears to Mary Magdalene

Mark 16: 9-11; John 20: 11-18

Mary Magdalene, recognising Jesus as he calls her by her name, is about to throw her arms round his knees in an upsurge of exuberant joy. But the old relationship is over: Jesus sends her off to the city to tell the disciples that she has seen the Lord, who is now on his way "to my Father and your Father, to my God and our God", voicing in a nutshell the tremendous content of the Good News of salvation.

'Woman, why are you crying?'

John 20: 13

Questions for discussion

What makes you upset?

Who helps you to feel better?

How do you feel when you see someone after a long time apart?

Why is Jesus a special friend to you?

What Good News can you tell other people about Jesus?

The sun is beginning to set. Watch the sky as it changes colour. You are on the way to Emmaus.
You have been walking for several hours. You haven't noticed the time because you have been talking to one of the disciples.
You have been talking about Jesus. Since he died you have been feeling very alone and wondering what will happen next.

As you walk a stranger joins you and asks you what you are talking about.
You are amazed. Surely everybody knows about Jesus of Nazareth!
Tell the stranger the story of Jesus.
Tell him how you became a special friend of his.

The stranger seems to know more than you do. Listen as he starts to explain to you things that you have never understood. Somehow it is hard to listen.
Your heart is beating fast. Who is this man?

As you get near to the village you suggest to the stranger that it is time to rest.
You want him to stay with you. Somehow you know that he has more to teach you.

You find a table in the inn and sit down. The stranger takes bread and blesses it. You close your eyes and you can hear the voice of Jesus, yes, you can hear the voice of Jesus back in the Upper room, "*Blessed are you, Lord God of the universe.*"

This surely is Jesus! You open your eyes but he has vanished!

You leave the inn and return to Jerusalem. You must find the other disciples.
You must tell them that it's true – Jesus has risen. You find the other disciples and tell your story. What did they say to you?

9 *The disciples of Emmaus*

Luke 24: 13-35

The radiance of the setting sun surrounds the three figures. Jesus is the Sun who knows no setting (cf. *Isaiah 60: 20*), he is more radiant than the sun (cf. *Wisdom 7: 29*). In a few minutes the disciples will recognise him at the breaking of the bread and know that his radiance has set their hearts on fire. Running back to the city they too become his witnesses.

'The Lord is risen indeed!'

Luke 24: 34

Questions for discussion

Have you been on any journeys?

Where did you go and who did you meet?

Can you remember times when Jesus was important in your life? When were they?

How do we remember Jesus' life?

How can you show Jesus you remember what he has done for you?

You've been out all night fishing. You haven't managed to catch anything. As you lowered your net for the last time you were thinking about Jesus and how different thing are without him.

Think back to the day when he called you. He told you to follow him and he would make you a fisher of people.
You did follow him. You didn't know where he would lead you.
You didn't know that he would have to die.
Pull in your empty net and head for the shore.
There's somebody standing there. He doesn't look like a fisherman.
What does he want?

He asks you if you have caught anything. There's something about his face that you recognise. Have you seen this man before? He smiles and tells you to throw your net out again. The way he smiles reminds you of Jesus. You start to think about Jesus and don't realise that your nets are full and about to burst.
One of the other disciples recognises him and shouts, "It is the Lord!"
You are so excited that you jump out of the boat and head for the shore.
You must see for yourself. Is this really Jesus?

Jesus has prepared breakfast for you. Sit down to eat the bread and fish he has cooked. Jesus keeps looking at you. Is there something that he wants to say?
The other disciples have started to walk along the shore, but you want to stay with Jesus. Jesus turns to you and says, "*Simon, son of John, do you love me more than these others do?*"
Why is Jesus asking this? Doesn't he know you love him?
Tell Jesus how much you love him.
Jesus asks you the same question three times. Each time you give the same reply. Now Jesus turns and looks at you and you remember the way he looked at you when he asked you to follow him.

Jesus says those words again, "*Follow me.*" What do you answer?
What will it mean this time?

10 Breakfast on the seashore

John 21: 1-14

It is striking that none of those who saw Jesus after his resurrection recognised him at first. He was different, and yet they knew it was him. The disciples are looking at him, bursting with joyful recognition but hardly daring to believe it. In the glow of the fire, in the twilight of early morning, they are on the point of vision, as they watch him in his familiar gesture of breaking the bread.

'Bring some of the fish you have just caught.'

John 21: 10

Questions for discussion

What does it mean to be a 'fisher of people'?

What can you do to follow Jesus?

Is it sometimes difficult to do what you know is right?

How can you show other people that Jesus is important?

How can you show Jesus you love him?

Jesus has told you not to leave Jerusalem. You have met together with the other disciples to find out what Jesus wants you to do.

Jesus is with you now. He tells you that you will be his witnesses to the ends of the earth. How will this happen? You are an ordinary fisherman from Galilee – you don't have any special powers.

You think of the times that you have listened to Jesus preaching.
You think again of the times you have heard him talking about the Kingdom of Heaven – a time when everybody will live together and really love each other.

You close your eyes and wonder what it will mean to be a witness to Jesus.
You feel a strong wind blowing and when you open your eyes Jesus has vanished.

Look up, the sky is filled with bright light. Clouds are racing across the sky.
Where has Jesus gone?

You turn around and there are two men in white standing beside you. They ask you why you are staring into the sky? You answer them and they tell you that Jesus has been taken up into heaven and he will return in the same way.

You talk with the other disciples and wonder what this means.

As you walk back to Jerusalem you think of the time that Jesus appeared by the lake. You think of his words, "*Follow me.*" How can you follow Jesus now?

11 *The Ascension*

Mark 16: 19; Luke 24: 50-53; Acts 1: 1-12

Luke's account in Acts suggests a visible ascent, a going up into the clouds, watched by the disciples, a description reminiscent of Elijah's ascent, watched by Elisha (cf. *2 Kings 2-9*), who was promised a double portion of his master's spirit if he could see him going up. So it was with the disciples: they received the Spirit not long afterwards. The cloud is a biblical image of the presence of God, as on Mount Sinai (cf. *Exodus 24: 15-18*) and at the Transfiguration (cf. *Matthew 17: 5*).

'They worshipped him and went back into Jerusalem, filled with great joy.'

Luke 24: 52

Questions for discussion

Have you ever said goodbye to a friend knowing you will not see them for a long time?

How do you think the disciples felt when they saw Jesus for the last time?

How can you be a witness for Jesus?

How can you spread the Good News of Jesus' life and death?

What do you think the Kingdom of Heaven will be like? Can you describe it?

Imagine you have gathered with the disciples to celebrate the feast of Pentecost. You have been praying together. Listen carefully, it sounds as if there is about to be a violent storm. You know the sounds so well and you know that it means danger when you are out in a fishing boat.

There is a wind blowing through the room in which you are sitting.
Something strange is happening.
Your head is starting to spin and all around you the air feels very warm.

Close your eyes and you can hear the sound of people speaking in several different languages. Open your eyes and you see that it is your friends. They are praying aloud in many different languages.

Follow the disciples out into the street. They are still praying aloud. Watch as crowds of people start to gather. These people come from many different areas and they can all understand the disciples.
This really is a miracle.

So this is what Jesus meant when he said that you would be his witnesses to the nations. The Holy Spirit has come as Jesus promised. You knew that Jesus would keep his promise.

The crowds are still gathering and all the disciples are talking about Jesus and the things that he promised. A crowd has gathered around you. Talk to the crowd and tell them what you know about Jesus.

12 The Descent of the Holy Spirit

Acts 2: 1-13

Glowing reds and yellows dominate this poster: movement, tongues of fire, a strong driving wind, joy and transformation, ecstatic excitement: Jesus' promise is being fulfilled. With the disciples are Mary, the Mother of Jesus and some women who had been waiting and praying with them (cf. *Acts 1: 4*). Here too fire and the noise of the elements recall the events of Sinai (cf. *Exodus 19 and 20*)) and the passing of the Lord by Elijah's cave (cf. *2 Kings 19: 11*). Great things are happening! The small group of fearful disciples are instantly transformed into bold and fearless witnesses of Jesus, and soon the crowds will come flocking into the Kingdom of God, from all nations, peoples and races. "The Spirit of the Lord fills the whole world" (*Wisdom 1: 7*).

'They were all filled with the Holy Spirit.'

Acts 2: 4

Questions for discussion

How do storms make you feel?

Can you think of anything else which shows us how powerful nature is?

How can you pray with your friends and family?

Jesus kept his promise to you. Is there a promise you can make to Jesus?

What is the message that Jesus wants you to give to other people?

What or who will help you to live as Jesus would have wanted?

Teaching guide

At McCrimmons we recognise that planning with today's popular R.E. programmes is often a difficult and time-consuming task. This brief guide has been written to help you make the most of these posters without having to spend a long time looking for resources and information.

Here I Am & Walk With Me

The table on the opposite page is cross-referenced to the themes in the *Here I Am* and *Walk With Me* catechetical programmes. If you are short of time, we hope the table might provide a quick solution for teachers and catechists who are under pressure of work. The bold headings at the top refer to the stages of the R.E. programmes.

General themes

We have also included some general themes (under the *Others* heading) that may help you integrate the posters into other R.E. programmes. You may also want to adapt the posters and booklet material to suit the individual needs of your own school or parish.

Developing the material

If you have the opportunity, we recommend that you spend more time developing your own thematic index that suits the needs of your own unique situation. All the best R.E. teaching comes when the teacher or catechist has really thought about the needs of the children concerned and planned well with those needs in mind. We hope this table will be a useful starting point.

JESUS, OUR WAY (2)	N/R	ONE	TWO	THREE	FOUR
Entry into Jerusalem *Mt. 21:1-11*					Death/New life Growing
Cleansing of the Temple *Mt. 21:12-13*					
The Last Supper *Mt. 26:17-29*		Meals	Meals, Self-giving	Thanksgiving, Memories	Meals, Memories Self-giving
The Washing of the Feet *John 13:1-20*					
The Agony in the Garden *Mt. 26:36-46*					
Jesus is Arrested *Mark 14:32-52*				Death/New life, Growing	Death, New Life
The Resurrection *John 20:1-9*	Self Giving, Death/ New life, Good & Evil		Self Giving, Good and Evil, Growing	Death/New Life, Good and Evil, Growing	Growing
Jesus Appears to Mary Magdalene *John 20:11-18*					Good News
Emmaus *Luke 24:13-35*			Memories		
Breakfast on the Seashore *John 21:1-22*					Holidays/ Holy Days
Ascension *Acts 1:1-11*	Good News		Energy	Good News	
Pentecost *Acts 2:1-13*	Good News, Messengers Witness; Energy Holidays/Holydays	Good News, Energy Messengers/witness Holidays/Holydays	Good News Messengers/witness Holidays/Holydays	Good News Holidays, Holy days	Good News, Energy, Holidays Holydays

Jesus, Our Life poster series

THE BENEDICTINE NUNS OF TURVEY ABBEY

Part 1 **Jesus, Our Light**

This set of 11 posters that tells the vivid story of Jesus' early life. These posters are ideal for use during Advent and Christmas.

11 Full colour laminated posters / Size: A2 / Ref: LOC1P
Includes double panel Nativity poster (A1)

Part 3 **Jesus, Our Hope**

In this set of posters based on the life of Jesus, we follow the Ministry of Our Lord in the colourful depictions of his miracles, parables and other events, which build our faith and lead us in hope.

12 Full colour laminated posters / Size: A2 / Ref: LOC3P

God's Promise

A set of posters illustrating the power of the Old Testament. Starting at Genesis with a vibrant depiction of God's Creation and on to God's Blessing to Abraham and his people. Exodus follows with Moses receiving the Ten Commandments and then to Joshua and the story of the Promised Land. This colourful poster set carries on to illustrate some more of the fascinating stories from Scripture.

12 Full colour laminated posters / Size: A2 / Ref: POT1

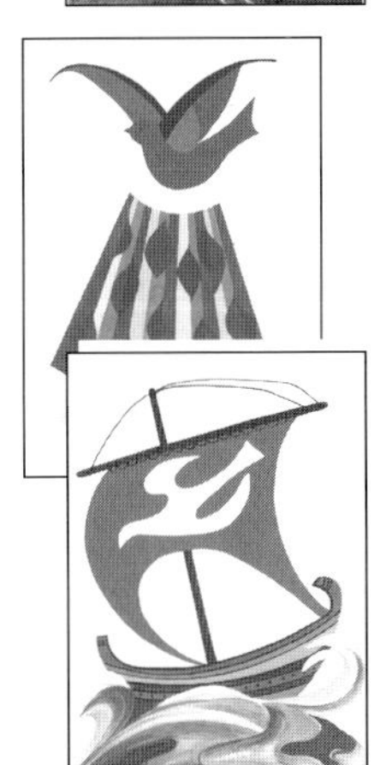

1 Breath of the Spirit
2 Spirit Alive

SISTER SHEILA GOSNEY

Two striking sets of posters. The first is an ideal resource for confirmation programmes, the second expresses the external imagery of the Holy Spirit – Fire, Wind and Water the Dove – and other symbols of the life of the Christian church. Each poster, with the help of an accompanying booklet, may be used to explore the messages of the Scriptures.

Breath of the Spirit
8 Full colour laminated posters and guide booklet / Size: A2 / Ref: MPCP1
Spirit Alive
8 Full colour laminated posters and guide booklet / Size: A2 / Ref: MPSA

The Footsteps of Christ

THE BENEDICTINE NUNS OF TURVEY ABBEY

This popular set has been created from 16 glorious oil paintings by the Benedictine Nuns of Turvey Abbey. Suitable for Lent & Easter, the posters follow Christ along the journey of the Cross from Peter's denial to the entombment and ending with the joy and hope of the resurrection.

16 Full colour laminated posters (includes FREE book) / Size: A2 / Ref: FOCP